Take A Dam Tour!
A Kid's Guide To Hoover Dam, Nevada

Photography By John D. Weigand
Poetry By Penelope Dyan

Bellissima Publishing, LLC
Jamul, California
www.bellissimapublishing.com

copyright © 2010 by Penny D. Weigand and John D. Weigand

All rights reserved. No part of this book may be
reproduced or transmitted in any form or by any means,
electronic or mechanical, including photocopying,
recording, or by any other means, or by any information or
storage retrieval system, without permission from the publisher.

ISBN 978-1-935630-05-0

First Edition

For Kids Who Love To Explore
And For Parents Who Love
To Explore With Them!

Take A Dam Tour!

Bellissima Publishing, LLC

Introduction

During the depression; thousands of men brought their families to Black Canyon to tame the Colorado River. In less than five years the largest dam of its time was built. Many lost their lives during its construction. Today Hoover Dam is a National Historic Landmark. And the American Society of Civil Engineers named it one of America's Seven Modern Civil Engineering Wonders! So take a dam tour with John D. Weigand and Penelope Dyan as you explore the pages of yet another great travel guide for kids!

The Bureau of Reclamation began conducting tours through the Hoover Dam and power plant in 1937. The Dam is ever changing and today they are constructing a bridge over the dam that looks like in itself, it is another wonder! If you want to visit Hoover dam and see what makes it work, it is located 30 miles southeast of Las Vegas on US Highway 93 at the Nevada-Arizona border.

The Hoover Dam tour is interesting and fun and there is a lot a kid can see, learn and do at the Hoover Dam. The tour guide will take you on a exploration of the tunnels and pipes and all the things electric and explain exactly how this mighty wonder works as well as why it was built!

Taken with ambient light, John D. Weigand again captures the essence of a fun place for kids and parents to see and visit, while Penelope Dyan tells its story with her whimsical poetry.

The sites of Hoover Dam are astounding, a tribune to the hardworking workers of America, and when you leave, you leave wondering how so much water ever found its way into the Nevada Desert! But you are glad it did!

Take A Dam Tour!
Bellissima Publishing, LLC

Take A Dam Tour!
A Kid's Guide To Hoover Dam, Nevada

Photography By John D. Weigand
Poetry By Penelope Dyan

When you drive to Hoover Dam,
you will see it is quite an unusual place,
It looks sort of like something
from the great vast outer space.
And you think you might have been
transported from way off afar,
As you sit there asking "Are we there yet?"
from the back sit of your car.

You see a monument of a man scaling a wall,
And he's made out of cement or something
heavy, so you hope on you he won't fall!

And you also notice something funny. . .
daises in the desert, looking so warm and sunny.

And then as unusual as it may seem, right there in the desert is a whole bunch of green!

And as you look all around you
at the daisies and the green
You see a tall tower that really does lean!

You can see something old...

And a bridge that is new.
They're building a bridge near the dam
And here it isn't quite through!

There is a trading post,
a shop where you can buy toys,
And lots of other things
for moms. dads, girls and boys!

To the Hoover Dam tours
signs point the way,
where you can tour and have fun
just old day.

Inside the dam engineers work
to keep things tight.
They rebuild the generators when they need to
so everything's right.

And here are the generators
all in a row,
making electricity as they hum,
as you may well know.

And then you see a tunnel...

And another tunnel too!

And some tunnels you can go into,
and some you can't go through!

Of this tunnel you might be wary.
Because there's a sort of a bridge,
and it is really quite scary.
In the dam you will see tunnels galore. . .

Some you can't go into. . .
They have a locked gate or locked door!

This is a generator.
It works day and night.
Because for the dam
it provides workers with light!

And when you are done with
your big dam explore,
there hangs that monument
where it hung as before. . .
And in the background,
you'll see that new bridge,
that is near the dam
and spreads ridge to ridge.

And below an american flag you can read,
about the men who met our need.
For our great country
they had a dream and a mission,
and they built for all of America
an amazing vision!

And as the sun sets among the black clouds
in the dark desert sky,
you will remember and wonder
as you say good-bye. . . .
You will ask yourself how this was ever done,
out here in the desert beneath the hot sun.
And then you will remember
that as impossible as it might seem,
it was about some men who
simply followed a dream.
And they left a message here
just for you,
And that is that your dreams
and your visions really can come true.

Lake Mead in the desert. . .

Who would have ever thought that in the desert there was so much water?

There is never an end to a dream or a vision,
especially if you make it come true,

www.ingramcontent.com/pod-product-compliance
Ingram Content Group UK Ltd.
Pitfield, Milton Keynes, MK11 3LW, UK
UKHW060137240426
12048UKWH00002B/78